fourteen poems

Issue 14

First published in 2024 by Fourteen Publishing.
fourteenpoems.com

Design and typeset by Stromberg Design.
strombergdesign.co.uk

Proofreading and copy editing by Lara Kavanagh.
lk-copy.com

Printed by P2D Books Ltd, Westoning, Bedfordshire, UK.

ISBN:
978-1-7384871-3-4

Hello everyone,

Welcome to Issue 14 of *fourteen poems*, our celebration of contemporary queer poetry!

There's something particularly magical about hitting Issue 14, not just because of the numerological feel behind it. It now means we've published almost 200 queer poets, from established to new ones. I'm thrilled that you're here for the ride alongside us.

As always, I'm excited about our new batch of fourteen poets and can't wait for you to fall in love with their work. Through the editing process, I get to really sit with all these poems and thoroughly engage with them, which is such a special feeling. There's this beautiful moment before the books fly out into the world where I really get to deep dive on each of these little beauties. I can't wait for you to do the same once you open these pages.

There's a lot of love in these poems this time around. There's the lyrical longing of Billie Manning's "not texting you is like a sandpaper wank", which depicts that rush of a new crush so perfectly. And then the sexy, swooning romance of Laurie Eaves' "apronstrings", with its playful language bouncing around the page like a polka.

And then there's the other side of love. Liz Quirke's "To the woman who told me my wife was having an affair" manages to balance all the narratives spinning around a betrayal, while Adam Panichi's "Concrete Quarterly" looks at a potentially toxic love, with the concrete symbolising the speaker being increasingly dragged down by its weight.

When you combine that with the family love of Stanley Iyanu's "οἰκία [home]", the lyrical and physical love of Kami Enzie's "Ode to Every Cumdump at 4 a.m." or the self-love glimpsed in Jemima Foxtrot's "Treasure", I hope we offer a broad range of ideas and stories.

And if one of these poems hits the spot for you, remember to head over to our Instagram where we feature the majority as recorded readings or live chats. As I said, I live with these poems on the page for so long, then always find something radically new when the poets read them out loud. Come join us over at Instagram.com/14poems.

Thanks for reading and I hope you enjoy these fourteen poems!

Ben, Editor

contents:

Liz Quirke is from Co. Kerry, Ireland and has published two collections of poetry: *The Road, Slowly* (Salmon Poetry, 2018) and *How We Arrive In Winter* (Salmon Poetry, 2021), which was a Poetry Book of the Year selection in *The Irish Times*. Liz has a PhD in Creative Writing (Poetry) with a focus on Queer Kinship in Contemporary Poetry from the University of Galway, and is currently a lecturer in Creative Writing at University College Cork.

Instagram: @quirkeyliz

X: @quirke_liz

To the woman who told me my wife was having an affair

though we never met   you parked yourself   neatly in my history

your language moved my body
from text   to subtext

before the first pawn slid   from the board

starlight and night echoes   superceded sex for me   long before

your missive   of where   my wife

had been

dagger to the breast   like falling in love

in   slow   motion

stop
motion

affair as swagger   as coffin screw   as empty diesel gauge *adagio adagio*   from gloved hand to armature

my skin pulsing concave   love pulled from tips of finger

before the slice

the print of your slap on my mouth

we held coffee cups in our palms   as she lied to me   at the train station

her name misspelled   like we were in some rom-com meet cute

shunt across the country   stone wall milch cow

who loves you   pretty baby   now all the boys of summer are gone

coraggio coraggio

two fingers in a glass   two fingers in my ribs   two   in her

box
room
battle worn b&b   rent-a-bed

stare
in the
window

an exercise in grief   in greed

my children   their empty beds

whether the tether survives still   she razed   the house

but your fingerprints   are all over   the bruised parts   of my body

Liz Quirke

Cal O'Reilly is a writer from Wexford, Ireland currently studying in Belfast. His work appears in *Cyphers Magazine, The Irish Times, Impossible Archetype, The Poetry Review,* and *Ink Sweat & Tears.*

Instagram: @cal.oreilly

Naming

after Remi Graves

I pull on names like shirts/ toss them like coins into the mirror/ the first person I say it to/ is a stranger with soft hair/ and a top-floor apartment/ back home I'm a waterlogged field/ my old name a drenched coat/ scrunched under a bus seat/ at work I count the times I'm called mate instead of love/ every day is just a placeholder/ until it isn't/ I don't know who I'm apologising to/ when I swerve muscle memory/ onto a track/ as softly gravelled as the throat I want/ body as forward slash/ transition or be forever in the next room/ trying to hear yourself think/ I catch my breath running/ the first time you say my name/ a feeling/ fills my chest/ like a room I can stand in/ so bright/ I don't need to look past it

Cal O'Reilly

Em Pritchard lives in Oxford, UK. They have poems published in various magazines including *Magma, The Rialto,* and *Oxford Poetry,* and have been a digital Poet-in-Residence for the Poetry Business. Their article on Frank O'Hara's Queer Trees was published in the *Cambridge Quarterly.*

Instagram: @books4gays

Something That Wants to Live

When I write about the heron
we saw above the pond, clean
and grey and graceful, chest
feathers fringing on a cowboy
jacket, how it dived in and emerged
so quickly with a fish in its beak

and flew towards us on the bank,
how we watched the fish twist
in the air, desperate, and how,
after the heron swallowed
we saw the fish move again
inside the heron's neck,

I'm writing about my fingers,
how they moved inside you
like something that wants to live,
how your mouth opened wide and
I put my eye to it, how I could have lived
inside the hollow of your throat.

Em Pritchard

Alyson Kissner is a winner of the Edwin Morgan Poetry Award and placed second in the 2023 Bridport Poetry Prize. She has also been shortlisted for the Rebecca Swift Foundation's Women Poets' Prize 2022 and twice shortlisted for the Scottish Book Trust New Writers Award. Her work can be found at alysonkissner.com.

Instagram/X: @alykissner

A list of physical experiments

- freezing is an act of preservation

  however impermanent

  a frog will see snow fall for the first time
  + forget the next day

  though its body remembers

  when you kissed me outside on the back porch
  I had snow in my hair

  + when the snow melted the hour after
  it could never be snow again

  only ice/only fever

  as always, it depends on how long
  we let each other's particles melt + condense

  i.e. how long my neck suffers exposure

- cf. boiling will kill the frog faster

  it won't need to remember
  the difference b/w hot/cold/childhood/hungry

  possessed/October/etc.

  while the apologue suggests that by heating the frog
  gradually

  the animal won't notice its death

  acc. modern biologists, a frog that's progressively cooked
  jumps out

ex. I bought you overpriced sandwiches
ex. I knew the water was hot but

I was afraid of living out in the open, i.e. of jumping out

into thin air

- gravity may not always keep things as they are
  but it returns its objects to their approx. places

ex. I think I jumped once
ex. I think I never stopped falling

Alyson Kissner

Isaiah Yonah Back-Gaal (he/they) is a queer poet, climate justice organiser, and drag performer from Brooklyn. They completed an MFA in creative writing at The Ohio State University where they served as Managing Editor of *The Journal*. Their work can be found in or is forthcoming in *Seventh Wave Magazine, Ghost City Review,* and *Copper Nickel* and has received support from the Greater Columbus Arts Council. You can find more of their work at isaiahbackgaal.com

Instagram/X: @isaiahbackgaal

Ask

Like any good door knocker, I've been trained
to make the hard ask. Your contribution.
Your vote. Your county of residence and soft
mattress topper. Permit me
your living room pull-out, your butcher paper and platform
shoes, we're going out asking and this is how you ask
for my hand. For my winking birthmark. Ask
for my coat. For some small inconsequential personal
detail: my social, my favorite shade
of lavender. My last lover's
mother's maiden name. Ask me
the temperature of the turkey baster
my mothers ferried home in a taxi. Here
my tongue. Stranger, spin me senseless
but don't kiss me without asking. Ask what
your country can do for you and what you
can do without a country. Ask for today.
Ask for a prophecy from the boy selling mints in the bathroom
and he'll say *See you next week.*
Ask for the dawn and you'll get it.
Don't ask me the last words I spoke
to my mother, we've only just met.
Ask me my occupation. Look around.
I'm not done speaking yet.

Isaiah Yonah Back-Gaal

Adam Panichi is based between the UK and Italy and has had work published in *I'll Show You Mine, VAINE, Dust, berlin lit, Atrium, Pulp Poets Press, And Other Poems, Strix,* and *Magma*. He was a runner-up in both the Ledbury and Brotherton Poetry Prizes and his debut pamphlet *Cupid, Grown* will be published by Broken Sleep Books in 2025.

X: @adampanichi

Concrete Quarterly

The straight boy in the high-rise flat kissed
like he was growing a pearl under his tongue;
to sleep beside him was to share a bed
with a brutalist building. The straight boy
was studying a degree for which his subscription
to Concrete Quarterly would likely come in handy,
and that would make his parents proud.
When we first fucked, I could tell at least once
he'd sunk a body part into wet cement, felt relief
from the blurred boundary. It was sexy at first,
the hewn, passable façade, his deep quarry of mouth.
How we love to fetishise things that cause us harm.
As he came, he recited the formula for concrete's
tensile strength so precisely, it betrayed a childhood
practicing in a mirror. I saw then, the straight boy:
Impossible Construction, uninhabitable, folding
back into himself. Found us lying in petrified sheets,
white dust on the places I let him put his hands.

Adam Panichi

Kami Enzie is a Vienna-born, New Orleans-raised, queer Nigerian-Filipino writer. His work has appeared or is scheduled to appear in *Black Warrior Review, Chicago Review, Common Place, Image, Michigan Quarterly Review, Obsidian, Oversound, Pangyrus, Passages North, Poet Lore, The Poetry Review (UK), swamp pink,* and elsewhere. An alum of the Tin House Winter Workshops, VCFA's Postgraduate Writers' Conference, and a 2023 graduate of The Iowa Writers' Workshop – as a Truman Capote fellow – Kami was also recently selected as the poetry contest winner of the 2024 Tennessee Williams & New Orleans Literary Festival.

Ode to Every Cumdump at 4 a.m.

Eventually skull meets floor.
Commit to stillness.
Absorb all work that has been done.
When air smells like oxygen,
without the laceknot of gas,
my heartbeat fills your mouth.
Breathe in.
It pulses through the quarry
pouched between your ears.
Deep breaths out.
Earth is the lowly planet not named after a deity.
Oceans stretch stained wrinkled sheets
across the flooding floors. The nameless
planet turns over again, not dead yet.
Everything must happen.

Kami Enzie

Jemima Foxtrot is a queer writer, performer, and theatre-maker from Yorkshire, living in Berlin. She has written and performed in several works for the stage and has published two collections of poetry *All Damn Day* and *A New Game,* both with Burning Eye Books. Her third collection of poetry, *Treasure,* will be published by Bad Betty Press in 2024.

Instagram: @jemimafoxtrot

treasure

the lake is treasure

lying back & smelling it   letting my bodyfat carry me   thankful

the water-snake wriggling the surface treasure

she changed my whole sexuality with a sideways hug treasure   turned me briefly into a peach

glowing jewelled reward   treasure

the way she monkeys me she's that celery green

reassure me   treasure   & I picked those raspberries the colour of her nipples

little treasure in my palm   the best I've ever touched   drupelets between

tongue & ridged roof of mouth

my time alone treasured   the sticks we brought back from hiking   a memory of blushing at a text

that he sent me   foolish treasure   when he called me his girl

she says it's a mixture of the patriarchy & hormones that lets me fall in love with lampposts

& it is   I'm treasure   my body floating on the lake

warm treasure   wet treasure   lying back & smelling it

Jemima Foxtrot

Laurie Eaves is based in London, UK and has had work published by Bad Betty Press, Broken Sleep Books, Fawn Press, *Ink Sweat & Tears, Dear Reader, Atrium Poetry, Poetry Rivals, The Primer,* and Allographic Press, among others. He co-hosts the Dead Darlings podcast and hosts/produces both Genesis Poetry Slam and the Vogon Slam. Laurie's debut collection, *Biceps,* is available from Burning Eye Books now.

Instagram: @laurieeavespoet

X: @mrleaves

apronstrings

grab my apronstrings in a summersmile grip
& my knot falls loose, pinch a stray
jumperthread, pirouette me
with a wrist twist, unstitch
my shirt seams, strip

stretches of yewbark
skin, sigh my rib bones to
lightcatch on dust, swirl the song
in my lungs, reach the beat at my centre
til soft in your palm you have my everything.

Laurie Eaves

Ahimsa Timoteo Bodhrán is the author of *Archipiélagos, Antes y después del Bronx: Lenapehoking,* and *South Bronx Breathing Lessons,* editor of *Yellow Medicine Review's* international queer Indigenous issue, and co-editor of *Movement Research Performance Journal's* Native dance/movement/performance issue.

Co-founder of the world's first transgender film festival, he organised the world's first transgender Arab roundtable dialogue for *Sinister Wisdom*. He has received scholarships/fellowships from CantoMundo, Macondo, Radius of Arab American Writers, Voices of Our Nations Arts Foundation, and Lambda Literary.

His work appears in Ireland in *Channel, The Galway Review, The Ogham Stone, Poetry Ireland Review, Revival, ROPES,* and *The SHOp;* in Northern Ireland in *A New Ulster;* in Scotland in *Causeway/Cabhsair, Gutter, Markings, Read This, The Red Wheelbarrow,* and *Reliquiae;* in Wales in *Envoi, Poetry Wales,* and *Prole;* and in England in *Brand, the delinquent, Fuselit, Iota, Magma, Other Poetry, Poetry Review, Polluto, Sable, Stand, Trespass, Weyfarers, and SMEOP Hot.*

Vault

Once soil we had. On land we existed, not just floated through sky. Once upon a time we had wings. Before they were clipped. Now we search for fossils of feathers, memories of how we tried to leave ground. Now float is all we do, now all we do is fear the gravity lessening, the last bits of soil we did not destroy, leaving. We fear we may hurtle into space. Some call us fallen, angels. Some think this our new hell, to float beyond the heavens. The moon ever closer, people have renamed it. This is not how we planned to reach there and new homes build. Perhaps one day our bodies will litter that soil, rather than the one we left and to which never shall we return. Once future colony, now tomb. Archive. Vessel for all who have floated. A final return to ground.

Ahimsa Timoteo Bodhrán

Stanley Iyanu is a performer and poet based in London, UK. His debut pamphlet *My Achilles* was published by Burning Eye Books in 2023.

Instagram: @stanley_writes

X: @writesstanley

οικια [home]

At the table, Mama makes trahanas. A Greek delicacy, she says. Oodles of soft pasta emulsified in a steaming hot bowl. It's what I imagine drinking a snail would taste like. Cloying yet refreshing. Mum smiled like the night sky, bright glistening lights in the corner of her eyes. She liked to be by her maker and cradle the good book like she cradled me times before. It's her "solace", she'd say. The one man in her life she believes. I think she searches for meaning in sadness as if to make sense of the inevitable and finality of things. Mama holds my hand and with a blank stare; she lets me know she's fine – and I don't know how to reply – so I hold her hand in silence. Sitting on the sofa watching Location Location Location and the dog holding court on part of the sofa, his throne scratched out, him, stretched out sleeping, paws spread akimbo, belly to the sky. Baba likes a sensible open plan kitchen with sensible being the operative word. Stable, reliable, the kind of thing to grow into like a jumper three sizes too big. He says it's like … one day toes stretch out in the direction of home, seeking roots to burrow deep in soil. Home is a plate full of pastitsio, crusty bread and feta cheese, crack of black pepper, twist of garlic and oregano. Once it was yam, egg, red soup and small meat on birthdays and times of celebration. Home is really wherever he is, where we sleep, the places we argue, had sex and had sex again. My love grabs a plate, fills it to the brim, brings us water and listens. As he tears the bread, piece by piece, savours its flesh and stares at me.

Stanley Iyanu

Billie Manning is a writer from Hackney, London. She is a Barbican Young Poet and her work has appeared in places such as *and other poems*, *Magma,* and *bath magg.* She teaches poetry courses at City Lit and elsewhere.

Instagram: @bills.bills.bills.bills

X: @billie_poet

not texting you is like a sandpaper wank

o bus stop kiss!
o kiss of orange streetlamp
and suburban wall frost
of my hands inside your vest
the warmth of your waist
between my thumbs o!
kiss like a small golden bell
struck by a meaning hand
the play of you
the way you
worry my lip like a tiger cub o
kiss with mist
afloat in the air
like the last
drop
of honey
o baby
bus stop
where we
hail a taxi instead
hold hands in the back and hope
the driver won't see us
and later in your single bed
i nearly die of permission
winter whistling in
through the badly-fit window
but until then
noses nestled side-by-side
like slices of breakfast toast
and already I know
you're gonna god damn fuck me up girl
just from the way you push me slightly
back onto that bright red bench

Billie Manning

Sydney Vogl currently lives and writes in San Francisco, USA. Her chapbook, *CRYBABY!,* was chosen by Chen Chen as the winner of the 2022 Cow Creek Chapbook Prize and published in 2023. She is also the author of the chapbook *CALIFORNIA IS GOING TO HELL* (November 2021, perhappened press). Previously, she won the 2021 Jane Underwood Poetry Prize and the 2020 AWP Intro Journals Project. Her work can be found in *Iron Horse, Jet Fuel Review, Honey Literary, Booth,* and more.

Instagram: @sydneyvogl

TWO MONTHS AFTER WE BREAK UP, I RUN INTO YOUR ROOMMATE

we are careful not to unpin the grenade
between us. i want to ask her everything i don't
know about your new life.
have you stopped drinking wine.
do you talk to a therapist now.
does she know my name.
have you developed a taste
for another girl. do you boil her
water on the stove. i bet she never cries.
i'm old enough to know i should
be afraid of ghosts. but tell me,
if my name is still tongued
into your clavicle. it's funny,
to see her here, like this,
because i only used to know
her when i was in love and wrestling
on the living room floor, waiting for
the kitchen timer to tell us something was warm
and ready to be scooped inside us.
i burned down the roof
of my mouth that night.
do my pupils look smaller.
i remember brilliant black holes of want,
or maybe they were violet
or maybe i was drunk
with the thought that i might collapse
into a life where there are no knives
hidden in coat pockets or behind fingernails.
do you actually believe that. after everything.
can you love someone without
first having a way
to destroy
them?

Sydney Vogl

Katie O'Pray is a non-binary, UK-based writer. Their debut collection *Apricot* was published in 2022 by Out-Spoken Press and their work has been associated with national and international prizes, publications, and institutions.

Instagram/X: @opraykt

At the town's first Pride

Queerness tracked thru June like grass
on a carpet. This month, plenty places
proclaim to be ours – colourful, camp, motives
obscured with glitter. My voice is clear when a fist
-ful of us share out a chant at the march, carrying
an inherited language, not the expected
disco tunes. Men with walkie-talkies catch
the scent of unrest, words that might antagonise-,
could scare the children. These rainbowed kids
that will soon be us, that we have been; born into
the disputes of England's unkempt gardens. Coppers
point us out, give a warning. This is our day
in their year. Our allotted sanctuary
for the afternoon. I don't think I'll stay
past dark, but my hands seem important,
holding up my share of patchwork
sky. Our bright bodies spanning the park
like a banner. Some girls are trading
hormones, 3 metres outside the official
gates. Boys pass down their well-worn
binders, pocket a bounty of hard-won
condoms. I don't mind how my flesh is
being read back to me. I greet everyone
as a likely friend. Mutual siblings. A lover once
removed. We're dressed up as caricatures
of ourselves. Cartoon things, striking against
the smalltown. On the way home, Pride
is a tinny party I hear slightly on the wind.
The roads aren't closed & there's a place for us
to get changed. A quiet in which to consider
where we live.

Katie O'Pray